> "Lay this unto your breast:
> Old friends, like old swords, still
> are trusted best."
>
> – *John Webster.*

# Contents

## Poetry

iStock.

## From The Manse Window

# Country Calendar

*Illustrations by Jim Dewar and Mandy Murray/Thinkstockphotos.*

spring

# Shawls Of Lace

A SUBTLE fragrance fills the air
And drifts among the trees,
As blossoms on their laden boughs
Are jostled by the breeze.
When sunbeams dance upon the blooms,
They're bathed in golden light,
And fragile petals brushed with dew
Seem frail and fairylike.

The trees are dressed in springtime's best,
In shawls of dainty lace,
And bridal petals flutter down
And touch my upturned face.
Then suddenly my heart leaps up;
I want to dance and sing
And shout in exultation
My welcome to the spring.

*– Kathleen Gillum.*

# Welcome, Spring Visitor

**I**T was always about the same time of the year
Our visitor arrived to stay with us here.
We never were certain of exactly the date,
For sometimes the weather caused her to be late.

She stayed for some months every time that she came,
And often we knew she'd appear dressed the same.
Her favourite colour at first would be green,
Which she'd love to show off wherever she'd been.

Then she'd flaunt yellow, blue, pink and white;
Wherever she went was a beautiful sight.
She was a true artist whose landscapes were pure,
Her skill was God-given, her efforts mature.

The birds, then excited, had known she'd arrive.
They sang and prepared, glad to feel so alive.
Frisky the squirrels, as hedgehogs unfurled,
It was time to stop sleeping and enjoy their world.

With her every step, warmth and hope filled the air.
Her presence brought smiles and delight everywhere.
Her visit arrived with a warmth unsurpassed –
For our visitor, "Spring", we could welcome at last!

**– Chrissy Greenslade.**

*Love letter t*

# Love Letter

**I**'D be lost without my mobile, and it's fun being online.
Instant hellos by e-mail are really very fine.
I'm certainly no dinosaur; it's great to text or tweet,
And yet, for all that, there's something especially sweet
About that little red van, stopping by the gate –
Seeing the postman coming; a short impatient wait.
And then that gentle "plop" as the post lands on the mat –
No message in your inbox could ever rival that!
And on birthdays or at Christmas, I'd find it very hard
To just see on-screen greetings and never get a card.
So, thank you, Mr Postman, you still can make my day –
Though I'd appreciate it if you took all those bills away!

*– Deborah Mercer.*

11

# The Price Of Dreams

**E**ACH won't come easily, I fear;
The price of dreams can be quite dear.
But count your blessings more than gold,
For with a dream you won't grow old.
The strategy is not to lose
That charmed path which you must choose;
No good to merely look and wait,
And simply leave the rest to fate.

To live the dream and see it through,
The price will always rest with you.
It may be just a word or deed
To help to make your dream succeed.
No good to stumble on the way
And leave things for a future day;
Once the strategy is blown
A dream can never stand alone.

Be it fame, or love or glory,
Success will tell the same old story:
Those who see, and work, and do,
Will live to make their dreams come true.

**– Dawn Lawrence.**

14

# Daffodils

IN spring, the brightest flowers I've seen
Are always dressed in yellow and green,
And every year I just can't wait
To see them by the garden gate.

They're in my pots and flower-bed;
The more there are, the more smiles spread.
And golden ones with orange eye
Capture hearts of passers-by.

For in abundance, daffodils,
In borders and on window-sills,
In gardens, parks, village and town,
Make it impossible to frown.

I look for them wherever I go,
From tiny shoots I watch them grow,
And every year my greatest thrill
Is to welcome the first daffodil.

For cheerfulness they are the best,
And every year they pass the test.
Now, very soon, they will appear,
For they know spring is growing near.

They're shooting, budding, even now.
It's cold, but they'll survive somehow.
They'll flower soon – oh, what a thrill!
My favourite flower – the daffodil.

*– Chrissy Greenslade.*

*from the Manse Window*

# A Season Of Beauty

**T**HE Victorian poet-priest Gerard Manley Hopkins had this to say of the time when nature wakens from its winter sleep.

"Nothing is so beautiful as spring –
When weeds, in wheels, shoot long and lovely and lush."

To me it is a beautiful description of the season, but I can imagine all of you gardeners giving a frown. Weeds are a nuisance at times. They stifle young plants, spread over the vegetable patch and encroach on the flower garden, taking over every empty corner. That is true, but many weeds have a loveliness about them.

This spring, up in North Yorkshire, the roadsides have been ablaze with yellow dandelions. Later they will turn into the clocks so beloved of young children who enjoy blowing off the seeds. Examine them closely and you will see that they are tiny masterpieces, wonderful creations.

Buttercups make another vivid splash of colour after the long, dark months of winter. Clover attracts the bees and appears in a variety of pastel shades. I recall searching in vain for a four-leaf clover as a small boy.

As a lad, I would pick the small daisies that dotted the lawn. Look at one and you will see that the bright orange centre and white petals are perfect. Somebody once said of weeds that they are only flowers that are growing in the wrong place.

Another delight in spring is to watch nesting birds, often flying about with leaves, pieces of straw or thistledown in their beaks to be used in the building process. During the war years we children used to go bird nesting. We never damaged them or took any eggs; the excitement lay in finding an unusual one. Those I remember most are a goldfinch's nest hidden in the branches of a lilac bush, a lark's nest, no more than a shallow scrape in a harvested cornfield, and a wren's with its domed top.

**O**NE of my great interests for as long as I can remember has been to search for wild orchids. They are beautiful spring and summer flowers and many of them are scarce.

Last year I tracked down plenty of early purple orchids, and spotted ones which are common. I also ▶

*iStock.*

---

**By the Rev. David Bryant.**

▶ found a quarry containing pyramid and bee orchids, which are more unusual. Most exciting was a solitary fly orchid hidden amongst long grass, beneath a heavy canopy of overgrowing trees. I looked it up in my flower book and it had the magic words, *Fly orchid – rare*. I kept thinking about it all that week.

Turn to the animal kingdom and the picture is no less joyful. Sometimes I take the country bus to our nearest town. It meanders through quiet villages, skirts moorland and passes fields of bright yellow rape and green, springing corn.

I looked out of the bus window one day and nudged my neighbour.

"Look, there's a pair of mad March hares."

By now half the passengers on the bus were peering out at the hares, which looked just as if they were boxing.

Springtime in the Kentish village where I grew up meant the arrival of the funfair. The war years had been a frightening time with bombs dropping, German aircraft filling the skies and doodlebugs being blown up by our aircraft from the neighbouring airfield. So it was a great joy to have peace again and to see the lorries, caravans and trailers trundling through the street instead of tanks.

There was a merry-go-round made up of animals. You would climb aboard a lion, a goose, giraffe or whatever took your fancy. There came a hiss of steam from the organ, a loud blast of music and a shout of "hold on tight there." Round and round we went, waving frantically to our parents, who remained on firm ground.

Then there were the swing boats, and we challenged each other to see who would dare pull the hardest and bring about the scariest ride. When we were a year or two older we were allowed on the bumper cars. The rules set by the funfair staff were strict: no crashing on purpose, and absolutely no head-on collisions or you would be grabbed by the scruff of the neck and thrown off.

Add to that candyfloss, ice-creams, balloons, toys to be won and watching the blacksmith smash the hammer down on the strong-man machine, and you can appreciate that it was a magical time.

At nine o'clock we were dragged away, tired, hungry and faintly protesting, wishing we could stay on till it closed at eleven o'clock. We went to sleep with the faint sound of the distant steam organ ringing in our ears.

Robert Browning sums up the meaning of spring very well in his well-known lines.

*"The year's at the spring*
*And day's at the morn;*
*Morning's at seven;*
*The hillside's dew-pearled;*
*The lark's on the wing;*
*The snail's on the thorn:*
*God's in His heaven –*
*All's right with the world!"* ■

March's birthstone is aquamarine.

# A Country Calendar For *Spring*

■ Native Americans call the month of March the "Worm Moon", because as the temperatures began to warm and the ground started to thaw, earthworm casts appeared, heralding the return of the robins and the last moon of winter.

■ March's flowers are violets in England, daffodils in Canada and hyacinths in Ireland.

■ Spring marks the start of six months of continual daylight at the North Pole – while on the other side of the globe, six months of darkness descend upon the South Pole.

■ The Hindu spring festival of Holi is also known as the festival of colours and love. It is an ancient Hindu religious festival which signifies the arrival of spring and the end of winter and is also an occasion for friends and family to meet up.

For two days in late March throughout India and Nepal, revellers sing and dance around huge bonfires, rejoicing in the victory of good over evil. The most eye-catching part of Holi, though, is the kaleidoscope of coloured powders revellers throw at each other, creating a living rainbow.

You'll know it's spring when you hear the dawn chorus. Every spring, male birds sing during the early morning to attract a mate. This tuneful warbling can be heard in gardens, streets and parks in the early hours from March onward.

"March hack ham
Comes in like a lion
Goes out like
a lamb"

**– English Proverbs, 1670.**

# The Promise Of Dawn

**P**AINT me a picture of skies crimson, glowing,
As far into space the sun sets them on fire.
A gift in farewell from the day in its passing –
Glorious colour, my soul to inspire.

Sketch in beneath them the waves ever tumbling,
Gently caressing the shore as they break;
Singing a song of a sea spun in silver,
With glittering stars in its wake.

Colour the memory of harvest moon rising;
A huge golden lantern to point out the way.
Night holds a loveliness safe in its dreaming
That cannot be seen in the cold light of day.

Write me a verse near the edge of the canvas;
Words to speak clearly of God's tenderness.
For He who gave light to both day and to darkness
Surely never would leave us comfortless.

God signs his name 'cross the world every sunset;
A reminder to all who are weary, forlorn,
To trust and believe in the light of His love for us.
It holds – as always – the promise of dawn.

*– Marian Cleworth.*

# It Would Only Take A Minute

**W**E all put off those little jobs to do, perhaps "tomorrow",
Thinking there'll be extra time that somehow we can borrow.
All that clutter in the loft – I simply need to bin it,
For as I keep being told, it would only take a minute.

Then there is the tool shed I've been going to clear for years,
To tidy all the forks and spades, dibbers, trugs and shears.
It could be an opportunity to rearrange and trim it,
For, after all, I'm reassured, it would only take a minute.

Although the order seems quite tall, but needed nonetheless,
I should paint the entrance hall, and the colour reassess.
But first I must remove the skin, that means I must re-tin it –
I'm told this simple little job should only take a minute.

So now I will concede defeat; the battle I can't win.
All my procrastinations have worn a little thin.
So I'll scan the Yellow Pages and all the experts in it;
To find the one I'm looking for should only take a minute!

*– Brian H. Gent.*

# *Life Goes On*

**T**ODAY I heard the blackbird sing
His anthem to the sun
And, Lord, my heart was lifted up –
New hope had just begun.
Today the trees that once were bare
Were dressed in palest green,
And I rejoiced in heart and mind
Such beauty to be seen.

Today as storm clouds moved away,
A rainbow arch appeared
And, Lord, my heart was lifted up –
The sadness disappeared.
Today I knew that life goes on
As nature wakes anew,
And I give thanks for life and hope,
And I give thanks to you.

*– Iris Hesselden.*

27

# A Refreshing Thought

WHEN friends ring the doorbell, I invite them in.
They know they'll feel welcome before we begin
To chatter, for they know that soon there will be
The question, "Would you like some coffee or tea?"

And what is the first thing we all think about
When we're at home or we're tired when we're out?
If we want to rest or to chat for a while,
What do we suggest which ends up with a smile?

"A tea shop! Let's stop; have a nice cup of tea!"
Or "The kettle's just boiled. Come and have one with me!"
The comfort is there, always welcome to hear.
A cup so refreshing it fills us with cheer.

So, whether it's coffee or tea that we drink,
The warmth that it brings when you hear the cups chink
Is a hand out in friendship – welcome, sincere –
To make someone comfortable whilst they are here.

It's really a symbol of kindness and care,
An action of thoughtfulness, that we're aware
Of their need to relax, and our wish to please.
Our reward is simple – we'll both be at ease.

To be frank, I must make a simple admission.
Our invites for coffee or tea's a tradition.
It's cheering, refreshing, a cuppa's just right,
And whenever we offer, it's always polite.

*– Chrissy Greenslade.*

# The World Of Water Weed

**THE** footbridge spans a wide, clear stream
Which ripples gently on its way,
And looking down I love to see
The emerald tendrils bend and sway

Of sinuous, graceful water weed,
Where tiny minnows dart and hide,
And lazy trout with flicking tails
Cruise in and out and slowly glide.

And when the sky is overcast
The pebbles seem all dull and grey,
But if the sun should then come out
They gleam like jewels, bright as day!

Sometimes I see a dragonfly
With stained-glass wings come down to sip,
And swift fly-catching swallows, too,
Who soar and swoop and rise and dip.

I often lose all track of time
Just seeing the life down there unfurled,
That dreamy, silent, secret place –
The weedy depths of water world!

*– Eileen Hay.*

# When Love Was New

**W**HEN I see a sun-streaked sky
I think of days now long gone by,
When we went walking, hand in hand,
In our special wonderland.
When days were long and bright the view,
And you loved me and I loved you . . .
Then came those dreadful war-torn years,
With all the blood and sweat and tears.
We both took our separate paths,
And consequential aftermaths.
I often wonder if you see,
In mind, those days and think of me;
For now we're old with time to dwell
On far-off days we knew so well.
Those happy days 'neath skies of blue,
When we were young and love was new . . .

*– Brian H. Gent.*

# Grandmother's Gift

**G**RAN just loved to be creative –
Making things to give or sell.
I'd marvel at her careful work;
She'd such a gift, her crafts sold well.

Clothes for dolls and knitted blankets;
Scarves and jumpers, hats and socks,
And soft toys made from coloured fur
With bright eyes from her button box.

I loved those best of all, of course.
Then came the day when she began
To stitch together rich brown fur.
I asked, "What are you making, Gran?"

"A teddy bear," my gran replied.
I still recall the wondrous glee
Of holding him, complete and plush,
And hearing he'd been made for me.

He sat beside me while I played;
He shared my pillow as I slept.
His soft fur dried my childish tears;
Years passed, and still he's loved and
kept.

His sparkling button eyes have faded;
Fur no longer dark and rich.
Yet I recall just how Gran made him –
With her love in every stitch.

*– Emma Canning.*

# Eternal Spring

**O**FTEN in church, the words of the service are so familiar that we don't really think about them.

The other day I was at a communion service and when we reached the prayer of consecration and Jesus's words about the bread and wine, I found myself thinking about how much life had changed for the disciples as they shared that Passover meal with Him.

I imagined them reflecting on how far they'd come in the past three years. Normally they would have celebrated the Passover with their families, but home and family had been left behind a long time ago. Sacrifices had been made on their families' part, as well as their own, to follow Jesus.

I considered the fishermen whose lives had been clearly marked out before they met Jesus: it was all about business and family, and that was the way it was going to be. Life held no major surprises, everything was mapped out. Maybe they looked back that night and pondered on how far they'd come, how many unforeseen,

earth-shattering changes had taken place in their lives.

Of course they were about to face the greatest change of all – the death of their master, who they believed was the Messiah. And that would be followed by the even greater event of Jesus's resurrection, contrary to all human understanding and experience (although they had witnessed the resurrection of Lazarus, they were no doubt still trying to get their heads around that one).

We often don't like change, preferring things to stay the way they are. I think of Peter's response to Jesus when he says he's going to Jerusalem where he'll be handed over to the authorities and killed. To paraphrase what the gospel accounts say: "What, are you mad? Things are going great and can only get better. Stop talking rubbish!"

And yet things change and we can't stop it. Some changes are eagerly anticipated. I love waiting for spring. I love February and March, not for the months themselves but for that delicious feeling that so much lies ahead – warmth and sunshine,

*By the Rev. Susan Sarapuk.*

bluebells in the woodland and the dawn chorus, the Chelsea Flower Show and Wimbledon. Anything seems possible. Yet other changes are resisted or dreaded and sometimes can be overwhelming.

Change is inevitable; we can either face it alone, afraid of where the next blow is going to come from, or we can face it with God, knowing that He is unchanging and that He can be a place of refuge and security. You see, ultimately, eternal life is going to be eternal spring and that's something to look forward to.

There will be no more yearning for April and May and feeling sad when June comes, because it's a whole year before you can see bluebells and leaves unfurling on the trees again.

That first Easter was a mixture of utter despair and unbelievable joy, from wondering at the change in their lives, starting with the successful days of teaching in the temple, to sharing the Passover as one of the privileged inner circle, to the arrest in the garden, the scattering and the hiding in fear after their leader was crucified. How could things have changed so quickly and where was God now?

We've all been in the position where life is coasting along quite nicely and then something comes along out of the blue and stuns you. Suddenly the God who seemed so close, so reliable, is no longer there.

"Why could He let this happen?" you might ask. You might go further and wonder "Is there a God?". We realise how unpredictable life is. If there is no God then life is random and often cruel and unjust.

How bitter the disciples must have felt that such a good man who never did any harm had been so cruelly taken from them. They thought they were going to change the world together, but the might of civil and religious power had come down upon them and squashed the hope and the dream.

So who was Jesus if he could be so brutally silenced? What of everything he'd said and promised? Did it mean nothing? Apparently so. What were their lives going to be about now?

Maybe they would just go back to where they'd come from – rejoin their families and occupations if they weren't hunted down and imprisoned or killed themselves – and spend the rest of their days remembering what might have been and recounting the tales of how they'd spent three years with the preacher and miracle worker. "Why would God let this happen?" they, too, might have asked.

"Look how far we've come, but for what?" They were without God, they were bereft. This was a change they hadn't anticipated and it had knocked them sideways.

Then Easter day came. Mind boggling, impossible but true. Overwhelming joy. One thing it meant was that God would never leave.

"I will never leave you nor forsake you," Jesus had promised them. "I am with you to the end of the age," he was to promise them at the Ascension. They knew from then on, no matter what, no matter the changes in life that came their way, all would ultimately be well because Jesus was with them.

And so it is for us. We can look back on our lives and wonder at how far we've come, at the things that have happened to us, both good and bad. Sometimes, as I reflect, I wonder on how God led me into the kingdom when I was a student and then led me to ordination 12 years later.

There will be more changes ahead, but one thing is certain: because of Easter we will never be alone. The Unchanging One will walk with us if we let Him. And in the kingdom, spring will last for ever. ▉

# A Country Calendar For Spring

■ Spring means parsley and chives are back in season and we can look forward to lots of fresh flavour! Did you know that parsley is the world's most popular herb?

■ The tradition of spring cleaning may have started in China, where houses are scrubbed from top to bottom in preparation for the Chinese New Year, which is also the country's main spring festival.

■ Spring fever really exists! The increase in the amount of sunlight and rise in temperature triggers a natural surge in energy and happiness levels. However, for some people, it has the opposite effect and they feel weary and tired.

*"Spring is the time of plans and projects"*

**– Leo Tolstoy, "Anna Karenina"**

■ National Smile Month starts in May.

■ 2011 was the warmest UK spring on record, with daytime temperatures averaging a balmy 9.2 deg. C. The coldest spring on record was 1962, when Britain's thermometers struggled to hit 6 deg. C. during the day, while the wettest spring on record was 1947, when the terrible winter was followed by over 330 mm of rain.

■ It's cherry blossom time. These pretty, pink-tinged white flowers are incredibly popular in Japan, where television weather forecasts include daily updates on where the cherry blossom is in full bloom, with cherry blossom viewing parties in parks and woods.

# *The Oak*

**I AM** standing in your cities;
I am part of country halls.
You can eat upon my tables;
You can climb over my walls.

My roots are wrapped in history;
My arms embrace the sun.
I am shaped and smoothed and softened
By the things that you have done.

I am in your painted landscapes;
I am carved as modern art.
I'm the silent, wooden eagle
In the church within your heart.

I am driftwood on your beaches;
I am in your barns and beams.
I am fuel to light the fires
Of this nation and its dreams.

*– Susannah White.*

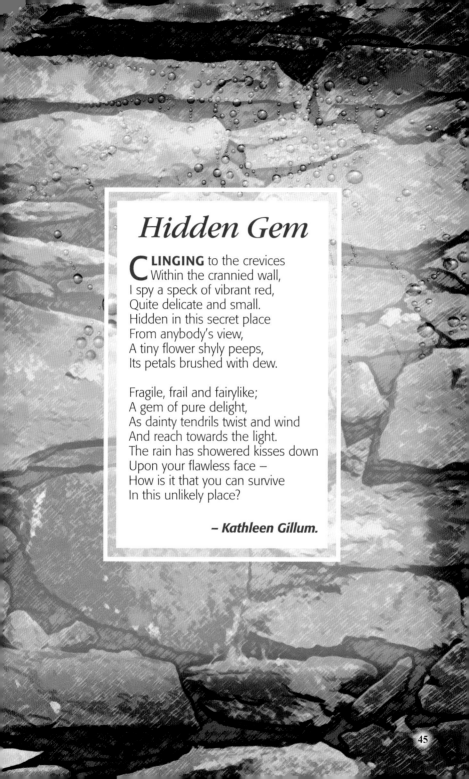

# Hidden Gem

**C**LINGING to the crevices
Within the crannied wall,
I spy a speck of vibrant red,
Quite delicate and small.
Hidden in this secret place
From anybody's view,
A tiny flower shyly peeps,
Its petals brushed with dew.

Fragile, frail and fairylike;
A gem of pure delight,
As dainty tendrils twist and wind
And reach towards the light.
The rain has showered kisses down
Upon your flawless face –
How is it that you can survive
In this unlikely place?

*– Kathleen Gillum.*

# *Round The Maypole*

THERE'S a maypole that's still standing on the village green,
But nobody remembers, nobody has seen
It hung with coloured ribbons that move in perfect time
Into changing complex patterns as the dancers intertwine.

But today, on May Day morning, in the early light of day,
I saw some local children who had come out to play.
They danced around the maypole, though they could not have known
About the old-time dance, so they made their very own.

And then just for a second, I caught a moment's glance
Of a group of merry ghosts who performed the maypole dance.
Yes, soon the vision faded; I just saw the children there,
But their laughter merged with birdsong and spring was in the air.

*– Deborah Mercer.*

summer

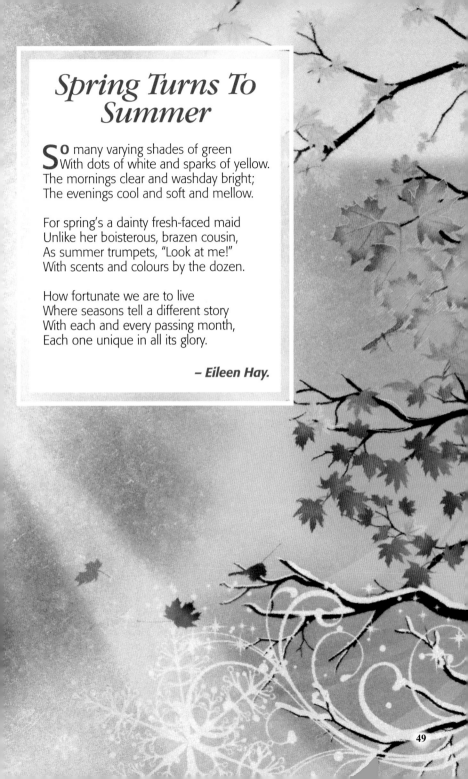

# Spring Turns To Summer

So many varying shades of green
With dots of white and sparks of yellow.
The mornings clear and washday bright;
The evenings cool and soft and mellow.

For spring's a dainty fresh-faced maid
Unlike her boisterous, brazen cousin,
As summer trumpets, "Look at me!"
With scents and colours by the dozen.

How fortunate we are to live
Where seasons tell a different story
With each and every passing month,
Each one unique in all its glory.

– *Eileen Hay.*

# Day Wakes

**T**HE morning sun rubs a sleepy eye
As fresh light floods an azure sky
With wispy clouds that float across
Like newly sugared candy floss.
A gentle breath wakes willow trees,
Kissed by a loving, caring breeze.
Birds sound their joyous wake-up calls
As cockerels crow from dry-stone walls.
Who could invent a better way
To wake a brand-new summer's day?

*– Brian H. Gent.*

# Transformation

**I LOOKED** in the mirror and what did I see?
Another year older and tired-looking me.
My eyes were half closed and still bleary with sleep –
How quickly I closed them when I took a peep.

I showered and dressed, taking care with my face,
And no longer I felt like a total disgrace.
I looked in the mirror, contented; I saw
A neat-looking, younger me, smiling once more.

I ignored all the birthdays that made me feel old;
I only let positive thoughts to unfold.
I saw the light shining in eyes that were mine,
And knew all was well and today would be fine.

With new motivation, intent surging through,
My heart filled with joy for this day which was new.
I opened the curtains, saw birds on the wing,
The robin and blackbird competing to sing.

I walked in the garden, perfume filled the air.
How young I felt then with spring flowers everywhere.
My neighbour's face brightened, she smiled as we talked,
A little child waved as with others she walked.

Plans filling my mind, I approached everything
With anticipation. What would this bring?
Contented and happy, my belief still was real –
Age isn't what matters, it's the way that I feel!

*– Chrissy Greenslade.*

# Dawn Celebration

I **LOVE** to rise and greet the dawn
At birthing of the day,
As darkness, on her slippered feet,
Steals silently away.
The sky is draped in robes of gold
Which lift the shades of night;
The sun streams out her radiant beams
In spears of dazzling light.

Cream and flame, then peach and mauve,
A blush of pink on grey,
The clouds awash with rosy glow
As colours interplay.
A symphony of vibrant tints
Is spread before the eye,
A kaleidoscope of colour is
All splashed across the sky.

A sudden stirring in the earth
And movement in the trees,
A little rustle here and there
And birdsong on the breeze.
There's signs of nature waking up –
A new day has been born,
As all of heaven blazes in
To celebrate the dawn.

*– Kathleen Gillum.*

# Music Of The Heart

**L**ISTEN, can you hear it?
There's music in the air.
The melody of love and life
Around us everywhere.
The skylark singing high above,
The wind sings in the trees;
The hum of traffic in the night
Is carried on the breeze.

The brass band playing in the park
On Sunday afternoons,
And in the city, buskers share
Their well-loved cheerful tunes.
The children singing in the church,
Their songs and hymns of praise;
Their voices lift a tired mind
And cheer the darker days.

Rejoice in all the sounds you hear –
Each note can play its part,
The melody of love and life –
The music of the heart.

*– Iris Hesselden.*

# *from the* Manse Window

# *In The Footsteps Of Greatness*

**S**OMEONE was telling me about a place they visited on holiday, where they saw a guitar signed by the legendary guitarist Jimi Hendrix. My friend was seriously impressed and kept saying how "awesome" it had been. He hadn't been born back then so this link with distant greatness seemed to excite him greatly.

Hendrix remains one of the early icons. A real innovator. Were he still alive, he would be seventy-five this year!

America is iconic. As a family we were privileged to visit Washington D.C. the summer after President Obama took office, and our children loved seeing the White House, even if we didn't meet the President himself. It was a little overwhelming just to be in some of the places we see on TV and to be near where some of the "history-makers" made history.

I mean, we were allowed to stand on the step of the Lincoln Memorial where Martin Luther King Jnr made his famous "I have a dream" speech in 1963. And yep, it felt awesome!

People have different ideas as to what constitutes "awesome", but

there's no doubt that travel sometimes gives us widely varying opportunities to come close to greatness. I can still remember the sense of wonder when my wife and I saw Michelangelo's *Pietà* in St Peter's in Rome. This poignant, life-size sculpture was completed in 1499 and portrays Mary cradling the body of Christ, after he has been crucified and taken down from the cross. It is the only work the artist ever signed. His genius may be appreciated when we realise Michelangelo did this work while still in his twenties!

Another opportunity for experiencing something breathtaking is the nearby Sistine Chapel ceiling and rear wall with their host of life-like figures painted by the same artist. It's recorded that Michelangelo didn't like painting nearly as much as sculpture, yet it is regarded as one of the greatest masterpieces in the world. Again there's no other word to describe it – it is awesome!

A slightly different brush with greatness was while on holiday in Geneva a couple of years ago. While there, we worshipped in an English-speaking Church of Scotland service, which was held in ▶

iStock.

*By the Rev. Andrew Watson.*

▶ L'Auditoire de Calvin – Calvin Auditorium, a building once central to the Protestant Reformation in Europe. While today's Auditoire has introduced a few modern facilities, as much of the original structure as possible has been preserved.

John Calvin and John Knox preached in this very same building in the 16th century. Their statues stand along with William Farel and Theodore Beza at the Reformation Wall in the nearby university grounds.

For those of us brought up in a Presbyterian tradition, these men were our spiritual forefathers in faith and practice. Greatly influenced by Calvin, Knox founded the Church of Scotland, with its then-radical form of church government using elected Elders. And 17th-century Scottish settlers in Ireland brought these new ideas with them, and the Presbyterian Church in Ireland was founded.

So yes, there was a sense of being close to something rather great and profound. For us, it was like touching bedrock. A kind of home-coming, especially when we sang one of the hymns to the Irish tune of "Be Thou My Vision", one of the pieces sung at my ordination as a minister around 25 years ago!

An interesting thing is how modern-day Geneva portrays these men and their Reformation as not just a spiritual revival of biblical Christianity, but much more. In their day they helped establish foundational social principles such as education, justice and democracy, on which much of the modern world is based.

On the wall of the *Auditoire* some of Calvin's inspirational principles are represented. Along with Reformation fundamentals such as "Grace alone", "Faith alone" and "Scripture alone", I was interested to read this:

"Fight for solidarity between all people. Resist evil. Invent paths of reconciliation."

In other words, John Calvin was not just a formidable theologian whose "Institutes Of The Christian Religion" remains a classic (and yes, awesome) textbook. He was a publicly minded pastor, caring for people, desiring everyone's highest good.

I'm reminded of some words of the Apostle Paul, another great theologian/pastor, who urged his 1st-century readers to strive for a godly balance of truth, righteousness and the "readiness that comes from the gospel of peace." (Ephesians 6 v 14 and 15)

Christians must practise and promote the highest spiritual and moral principles as taught by the bible, but we must also love and try to live peaceably with those who don't! Sometimes it is difficult. We may be misunderstood and misrepresented by opponents, but it is the way of our master, and we are to strive to walk in his light.

And here is something worth considering. While most of us may never have a following, see our work in a gallery or museum, or have our statue in the park, we can all move a little closer to greatness every day. We do so when we pray God's will for our lives in Jesus's name, and depend on the Holy Spirit to help us

practise the teaching of Scripture— like trusting in God's grace for salvation, seeking to become like Jesus in holy living and working to build a worldwide community of peace and love.

Crucially, we must do so not for our own fame or fortune, but all, as it says on the wall of Calvin's Chapel, "to the glory of God."

For in the end he is the one most worthy of the title "awesome". ▥

# A Country Calendar For Summer

■ The summer solstice on June 21 is thought to have been celebrated at Stonehenge for over 4,000 years.

■ Ice-cream was created for the Roman emperor, Nero. Slaves would carry snow from the mountains to Nero's kitchens, where it would be mixed with nectar, honey and fruit to make a frozen dessert fit for the emperor who would later fiddle as Rome burned.

■ Strictly speaking, watermelon isn't actually a melon – it's a type of berry. And the debate continues as to whether it's a vegetable (the watermelon is related to cucumber, squash and pumpkins) or a fruit (as it has seeds and a sweet flavour).

iStock.

■ Fuchsias, also known as Lady's Teardrop, are native to Central and South America, Tahiti and New Zealand. In New Zealand, there's a species of tree fuchsia which grows up to 50 feet high.

"It's a smile, it's a kiss, it's a sip of wine . . . It's summertime!"

**– Kenny Chesney**

■ In 1834, King George V provided the people of London with their very own beach at Tower Bridge. The beach was created by dumping 1,500 tons of sand on the banks of the Thames and over the next five years, half a million people enjoyed building sandcastles, playing about in rowing boats, relaxing in deckchairs and going for a paddle on London's Riviera! Fears about pollution closed Tower Beach in the early 1970s, but it opens to the public during the annual Festival of Archaeology.

# Daisy Chain

YOU made us a chain of bright daisies
   A thousand summers ago,
While the lazy sun blazed down on us,
Casting a mellow glow.
Petals, white as a wedding gown,
Opened in joy to its rays,
And the bees buzzed past, as we lay on the grass,
Dreaming of future days.

You said we were joined like the flowers,
But ours was a friendship chain,
So we linked our hands and promised
Lifelong friends to remain.
Now whenever I see summer daisies,
Although you are far, far away,
You're there in my heart, we're never apart,
As I remember that day!

*– Marian Cleworth.*

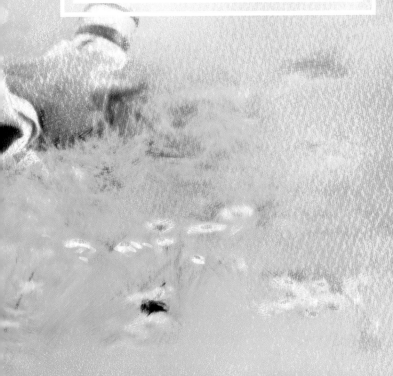

# A Time To Reflect

**I**'VE dug and weeded, raked and seeded,
Filled my tubs with glorious flowers.
I've potted seedlings, pulled out weedlings,
All of this in sun and showers.
I've mown and edge-trimmed, got my hedge trimmed,
Waged a war on grubs and bugs.
I've fed and nourished so things flourished,
Kept at bay all snails and slugs!
And now this treasure gives such pleasure,
I can take a moment's rest
To simply savour all my labour,
Feeling I am truly blessed.

*– Eileen Hay.*

# The Tide Will Turn Again

At times the world seems golden,
Everywhere a sea of peace
Where, cloaked in love and thankfulness,
Problems and troubles cease.

When lost in contemplation
Everything around seems green –
Alive, renewed, reborn again,
Our mind in tune, serene.

Then fears arrive to haunt us,
Causing ripples in the calm.
Thoughts tumble, threaten, weaken,
Causing turmoil and alarm.

This is the time to listen
To that silent voice within,
Then answers to our worries
And results will soon begin.

The reasoning power of quiet
Will now calm those restless seas,
And doubts and anger disperse
On a healing, balm-filled breeze.

The turning tide tranquillity
Laps gently on the shore.
Our faith and strength returning
To the golden days in store.

*– Chrissy Greenslade.*

# Beside The Sea

THERE'S nothing like a seaside trip
To brighten any day.
The salt sea air dispels all care
And blows the blues away.
There's nothing like the dancing waves
That swish around your toes;
The water's crash, the diamond splash,
Will wash away all woes.
There's nothing like a good cream tea
To make the world taste sweet.
Or twice as nice, a strawberry ice
Is just the perfect treat.
There's nothing like your own front door –
How fast the day has sped!
Our trip's been great, but now it's late –
Goodnight! It's time for bed.

**– Maggie Ingall.**

# *Paradise*

LOOKING through the rain-streaked window,
Elbows resting on the sill;
Summer's here – you'd never know it,
Looks like winter's with us still.

How I long for sand and sunshine,
Palm trees and exotic seas!
Coconuts and floral garlands –
"Another cocktail, waiter, please!"

But mine is no bikini body.
I wouldn't fit in on the beach!
I'd be lonely – first-class travel
Is beyond all my friends' reach!

I'll trade the cocktails for a cuppa,
Cake and chat at home again.
I'm not cut out for gracious living.
Life is better in the rain!

*– Ros McKenna.*

# A Chance To Dream

**I**F you'd like a chance to dream,
Sit by a gently flowing stream.
Listen to the water babble,
Let your toes in the coolness dabble.
Feel the breeze caress your face
And revel in the ripple's race;
Watch minnows swim o'er pebbled bed
And cheery trees their blossom shed,
Touched by the sunlight's dappled rays
As befits such tranquil days.
So, to dispel that furrowed brow,
What better time is there than now?

*– Brian H. Gent.*

# The Carousel

I WAS sort of talked into it.
She took me by the hand.
No good to tell Granddaughter "No" –
She wouldn't understand.
Most any kind of funfair ride
Will make me feel unwell,
But with a firm, stiff upper lip
I rode her carousel.

Not too bad, I thought at first.
I shouted, "Hold on tight!"
But then the music gathered pace
And that's when I took fright.
My steed flew round and round at speed;
I shot into the air.
I clung on tight with clammy hands,
My eyes glazed in a stare.

I had to concentrate so hard
To keep myself from falling.
I hardly heard wee Emily
Beside me, loudly calling.
"Look at me! Oh, Nanny, look!
I'm holding on one hand!"
I dare not let her see my fright –
She wouldn't understand.

And then at last the music slowed,
My steed slowed down at last.
With trembling legs I found my feet,
My heart still beating fast.
I found that I could hardly stand;
I shook from head to toe.
But Emily just smiled and said,
"Can we have another go?"

*– Dawn Lawrence.*

# A New House, A New Home

**S**UMMER is coming to an end and we are getting ready for the next chapter in our lives to begin. Happy New Year!

That might seem a strange thing to say, but it's not so strange when you realise for me and for many others in my church it is the start of the Methodist New Year.

At the end of the year (early summer, about June or July), the annual Methodist Conference meets and a new president and vice-president are appointed to preside over that conference and spend the year travelling around both at home and abroad representing the Methodist Church.

This same conference is also the opportunity for all the new ministers to be ordained, and they will join all those who have been ministers for many years and are preparing to uproot themselves from surroundings that have grown familiar to them (holding good or not-so-good memories), and moving their belongings and families to fresh pastures – whether this is the next town or the other end of the country

– in preparation for their new appointment to begin in September.

Several people I have come to know well are making preparations for moving. Of course, not all Methodist ministers will be moving in the late summer, as by far the majority are still living in the same manse, in the same appointment as before, simply because the congregation has invited them back and they are more than willing to keep working with the same familiar churches.

However, the unfamiliar holds new challenges which are appreciated by many people, and a new face may bring welcome changes at some churches that have become "stuck in their ways" and are still living with the same old routines that have been in place for many years.

There are advantages to living in a provided house, but there are also disadvantages as well, because ministers have to learn to live with the decisions made by previous occupants and they may well find that their prized possessions look out of place with the existing ▶

iStock.

*By Kathrine Davey, Mansfield Methodist Preacher.*

▶ colour scheme or expensive feature fireplace!

This dilemma is caused by the problems of having a "dual-purpose" house, which is both an important building in church life and a family home. It takes time to put your own stamp on a place, and there is always the fear that this will not be appreciated by those who will have to live in this manse in the future.

Of course, it is not just ministers who have to cope with the stresses of moving to a new house and area. There are a few people who have lived all their life in the house they were born in, but the majority of us have moved house at least once in our lives. When we last moved house, people were constantly asking, "Have you settled in yet?"

And the neighbours! Fortunately all those who live in our little cul-de-sac are very friendly; we all exchange Christmas cards and stop for a quick chat when we pass in the street, but you only have to notice the number of television programmes about problem neighbours and I realise I am extremely blessed in this regard.

Until quite recently, manses and vicarages were among the prominent houses in an area, but recently, with building space now at a premium, the church "goings-on" are frequently scrutinised by neighbours who live in very close confines. That reminds me of Jesus's words that we are to be "salt and light" in our communities, as we have a chance to let our values permeate society and effect a change – hopefully for the better – much as salt changes the taste of the fish and chips or the meat-and-two-veg that we eat.

God calls us to be a company of travellers and nowhere is this better seen than in this annual ministerial moving-day, when so many people have to settle into new situations at the same time. The people of the Old Testament were constantly reminded of their roots, as God commands them to recall "My father was a wandering Aramean", which was a reference to Jacob, who had wandered from Canaan to Haran and back and who later migrated to Egypt to join his sons who had gone before him.

Before moving house, I read some useful advice. The writer suggested having the kettle easily accessible amongst our belongings, and also to be able to make up the bed quickly, because we would be certain to find the process of moving tiring and would be glad of a comfortable night's sleep before the work of rearranging the furniture to suit our new surroundings really began.

However, Jesus did not have such comforts, which made me realise just how lucky I am. He told the crowds, "Foxes have holes and the birds of the air have nests, but the Son of Man has nowhere to lay his head."

His refugee status actually began when the young baby was forced to flee into Egypt with his parents to escape from the evil plans of King Herod, who tried to rid the nation of Jesus by killing all the baby boys in and near Bethlehem.

I am reminded of this every time I hear of people being forced to flee from a country to escape persecution, often having to face dangerous travelling conditions and being uncertain what welcome they will receive when they find somewhere to settle.

My own trials are put into perspective, and I realise how much I have to be thankful for. ■

# A Country Calendar For *Summer*

■ According to the Met Office, there were 669 hours of bright sunshine in the summer of 1977, making it officially Britain's sunniest summer.

■ In August, squirrels have their second litter of baby squirrels. The mother squirrel rears her brood, which can consist of anything from two to five babies, on her own until they're about fourteen weeks old, when they're usually able to fend for themselves.

*"All in all, it was a never-to-be-forgotten summer – one of those summers which come seldom into any life, but leave a rich heritage of beautiful memories in their going – one of those summers which, in a fortunate combination of delightful weather, delightful friends and delightful doing, come as near to perfection as anything can come in this world."*

**– L.M. Montgomery, "Anne's House Of Dreams".**

■ On the first Monday of August, Australians living in the Northern Territories celebrate Picnic Day – by going on a picnic!

"Great is the sun,
and wide he goes
Through empty heaven
with repose;
And in the blue and
glowing days
More thick than rain he
showers his rays."

**– Robert Louis Stevenson.**

■ Strawberries are the only fruit with seeds on the outside.

■ The world's largest rose bush is a white Lady Banksia which covers over 8,000 square feet. This spectacular rose bush is located in Tombstone, Arizona, having been taken to America as a small root by Scottish emigrants in 1885.

83

# British Trees

LET us praise our British trees:
Beech and alder, ash and yew.
Their voices rustle in the breeze,
Each year dying, then made new.

Let us praise the slender birch,
Known as the lady of the wood,
With shining bark and dappling leaves,
Her every aspect speaks of good.

Let us praise the king, the oak,
Spreading branches, growing slow,
Sheltering life in many forms,
His leaf-shade casts a greenish glow.

Let us praise the willow tree,
Maker of bats and screens and more.
Pliable; a healer, too,
Standing on the river shore.

Let us praise the tragic elm,
Once so common, now so rare.
Its green crowns stood against the sky;
Now it warns us – take more care.

Their voices rustle in the breeze.
A sound our forebears knew.
We must save our British trees,
Beech and alder, ash and yew.

*– Elizabeth Horrocks.*

# Petals On The Briar Roses

A S Mother Nature gently closes
Petals on the briar roses,
The sun turns to an orange glow,
Where softly swirling rivers flow.
Then, through half-closed sleepy eyes,
Furry creatures view the skies.
By mossy verge and bank they loiter
To start their nightly reconnoitre,
Disappearing in the night
Beyond the glow-worm lantern's light.
So daylight ends and softly closes
The petals on the briar roses.

*– Brian H. Gent.*

# Games Of Yesterday

**I REMEMBER** the magic of my yesterdays,
The simple enjoyment in so many ways,
When games that we played were made up in our mind,
Not digital or costly – the imaginary kind.

For outings in summer, down lanes we all went –
The countryside bursting with birdsong and scent –
With jam jars and fishing nets down to the stream,
For catching some tadpoles was my childhood dream.

Then cowslips and bluebells – a magical sight –
Could be picked, taken home for my mother's delight.
As books were so scarce, they were gifts I would treasure,
And dressing up, ball games and skipping, my pleasure.

We played in the fields when the long grass was mown,
Built houses – quite safe then to play on our own.
What halcyon days filled with laughter and fun,
The memories I have of long summers and sun!

My marbles and hopscotch, well-used whip and top,
With computer games now I know I'd not swap!
Pastimes are much different for children today,
But what games they would love from my yesterday!

*– Chrissy Greenslade.*

# Autumn Reflections

**S**WEET autumn days are here again,
Mature times of gladness,
Yet only yesterday it seems
Hares danced in springtime madness!
The new green leaves and shoots of May
Have turned a golden brown,
And scampering squirrels gather nuts
Where fledglings fluttered down.

A time to muse on work well done,
Of toil the seasons long,
The furnace days of summertime,
Sun mellows from here on.
In nature food all gathered in
To last the winter cold,
In man's brief span, time to reflect,
Fond memories growing old!

**– George Hughes.**

# *The Friend*

**I ASK** Old Bear whene'er in doubt, "I wonder, can you help me out?"
And Bear peers down with bright glass eyes,
That have this power to hypnotise.
Whilst I debate the "Why?" and "Where?", he fixes me with stony stare,
That leaves me with no doubt, at once, that I'm a veritable dunce.
He's rare in body, leg and limb, since only six were made like him!
So to his credit, I confess, he's quite a cut above the rest.

It's very comforting, I find, to have a friend who doesn't mind
However much I question him,
Who never thinks I'm slow, or dim.
He never seems to care at all that I am big and he is small.
I tell him all my tales of woe; he listens and just seems to know.
You cannot guess the cheer it brings, to just relax and tell him things.
No matter what the time of day, he sits and listens, come what may.

He may be just an old stuffed bear, but he's a friend who's always there,
Whose thoughts I never have to guess,
Who (almost) always answers "Yes",
But if I'm sure the answer's "No", I just agree – and tell him so.
We always talk of this and that. He doesn't mind how long I chat.
And here's another thought to prize: he never needs to exercise!
I wonder who else has a bear of whom they ask the "Why?" and "Where?"

*– Dawn Lawrence.*

# The Best Is Yet To Come

I'VE noticed signs that I am getting older.
My youth has flown, there isn't any doubt.
(These days, I'm getting into my pyjamas
Around the time the kids are going out.)

With children grown, it's time for an adventure.
Should I paint or draw, or take up the guitar?
Maybe I should bungee jump or wing-walk.
(I think that might be just a step too far!)

I've found the time for taking yoga classes,
I've even dusted off my silver bike.
I'm exercising everything but caution –
I'm old enough to do just what I like!

I've been assured the best is yet to come, still
Getting older has been quite a nice surprise.
There's just one thing I'm not entirely sure of –
Can someone tell me – when do I get wise?

– *Emma Canning.*

# It's Never Too Late

**IT'S** never too late to start again
In anything you do;
It's never too late to change your thoughts
If things are hurting you.
This moment is the time to heal
That broken, saddened heart,
To look for rainbows, ask for help,
And let your life restart.

This is the day to hold on tight
To all that you believe,
Then faith and trust will pull you through,
And doubts and fears relieve.
Hold on to life, forgive yourself
For actions in the past,
And you will find a brand-new future
Is waiting there at last.

Then you will find life can be good
And still times can be fun;
So leave the past behind you,
For your lesson's learned and done.
Grasp hope and positivity,
Reach out, let hope remain,
For now is the beginning
Not the end, so start again.

*– Chrissy Greenslade.*

# *Hair We Go Again!*

**I SIGHED** as I looked in the mirror;
The sight wasn't pretty to see.
I was having a really bad hair day –
Needed TLC ASAP!

I opened the door to the cupboard
And my eye spotted, *Special Shampoo:*
*Gives volume and body to fine hair.*
That'll do, if their promise is true.

I washed and massaged and I rubbed it
Into my scalp, as I thought
Of hairstyles that once I had flaunted,
Even though some had left me distraught.

My Afro looked like an explosion!
My poodle cut something from Crufts!
Italian Boy, urchin cut, mullet,
Gelled hair tweaked in hedgehog-like tufts.

Bouffant, bangs, beehive, back combing;
I tried these, and more, as I aged.
But now is the time for a new style.
I'm ready to start a new rage.

There! Shampooing done. Now conditioner.
(Oh, hair, you are having a treat.)
Next is the blow-drying process
When style will be finished. Complete!

Wrong. That's not the end of the story.
I looked at myself. What a shock!
My hair stood on end, soft and downy.
Oh, Lord! I'm a dandelion clock!

*– Thelma Moss.*

## from the Manse Window

# A Harvest Of Blessings

**I**T was John Keats who described autumn as the "season of mists and mellow fruitfulness". His immortal ode describes a progression through the season, from the maturing of the crops to their ultimate harvesting. It's at this season of the year that churches and congregations throughout the land hold their services to mark the gathering in of the harvest.

Sanctuaries are bedecked with flowers of every hue and decorated with fruits and vegetables and food products of every variety as they express their annual thank-you to God in prayer and in song at harvest thanksgiving services. God is praised and thanked for the fertile ground and for the miracle of growth, He is praised for the harvest of orchard and field, for the harvest of the garden and of the sea – not to forget the harvest that is quarried and mined: oil, iron, copper and coal.

It's at this time especially that God's people lift up their hearts in thankfulness to Him for, in the words of the harvest hymn, "All good gifts around us" which are "sent from heaven above"!

I rather think that the annual occasion merits the grander title, "Festival Of Thanksgiving" because that's in essence exactly what it is. People come together to thank God not just for the grain, the fruit, the flowers and the vegetables, splendid as they are, but also for the goodness in their fellow men and women, for cheerfulness, for laughter, for music and for song. Harvest thanksgiving must be extended to include all of these, too.

Indeed the spirit of thanksgiving shouldn't be reserved only for our annual festival of thanksgiving, but for every day of every week of every year. We owe God thankfulness, not for bodily nourishment only, but for all his gifts of grace. Thanksgiving normally goes hand in hand with cheerfulness – those who express gratitude are usually of a cheerful disposition because thanksgiving is an out-going and an out-giving of the spirit.

The prophet Joel penned these words long ago: "You shall praise the name of the Lord your God who has done wonderful things for you . . . and my people shall never be ashamed."

**By the Rev. Ian W.F. Hamilton.**

Shame eats into a person because it's weakening and debilitating, while gratitude or thanksgiving prevents such unhealthy anxiety from taking root.

The story is told of a man who was suffering a long spell of adversity. He was really going through the mill as seemingly every week some new blow hit him. As the months and years of misfortune passed, it got to the stage when he was beginning to dread the morning mail and the ringing of his phone.

His initiatives, his enterprises, they all came to nothing. As time went on, a sense of total failure began to overcome him. He lost any self-confidence he ever had, he avoided his friends, he was absolutely ashamed.

One evening, he was sitting at home with his wife, who had stood by him faithfully throughout his period of adversity. They together talked through his catalogue of misfortune, all through no fault of the man himself. After a lengthy discussion, with his depression sinking deeper and deeper, his wife suddenly said to him, "Instead of contemplating all the bad fortune you've had, why not think about some of your good fortune? You've had plenty of that, too."

She then started to spell it all out for her husband. His children were all growing up strong and fit, there had never been any serious illness in the family, they had paid off their mortgage and now owned their own house, and they lived in a delightful village.

What's more, despite all his setbacks, despite all his adversity, he hadn't actually crashed under it all. So far, he had coped.

"And we have some wonderful friends, too, and much more!" his wife added.

Now these things were all solid advantages, his wife went on to assure him. Things for which to be eternally thankful, and with all these behind him to support him he could surely carry on for a bit longer, and sooner or later he was bound to overcome all his misfortunes.

Life, for all of us, is sometimes like that, namely one moment of bad fortune or one calamity following another.

Frequently one misfortune seems to trigger off a never-ending stream of these and fighting back can be a terrifying and wearisome struggle, calling for infinite patience and inner strength.

However, if we're feeling shameful and sorry for ourselves, we're defeated even before we begin the fight back. If we meet the situation in a spirit of cheerful thankfulness for the blessings we do have, our battle back is half-won.

We just need to look around ourselves. There's always plenty to be thankful for and cheerful about. In the prophet Joel's words: "Praise the name of the Lord for the wonderful things he has given you!"

Yes, we have our plentiful harvest gifts and our beautiful churches and sanctuaries in which to thank God for these. But additionally we surely would want to thank God for his gift to each one of us of a life to live, a mind with which to think and understand, families and friends who love and support us come what may, for health and for health-care when we need it, for literature, for art and for

the sound of music. The list is endless . . . it's a harvest of blessings.

But not least we must "Praise the name of the Lord" for faith. For faith in an omnipotent, beneficent God who, in Jesus Christ, the Lord of the Harvest, has supplied and will continue to supply our every need.

The old chorus sums it all up so succinctly:

*"Count your blessings, name them one by one,*
*And it will surprise you what the Lord has done"*!

God pours out a harvest of blessings on every one of us, that surround us and support us day in, day out, and our response to our gracious giver can surely be no less than a festival of thanksgiving – every day of every season of every year! ▦

# A Country Calendar For *Autumn*

■ People who live on the Equator never experience the beauty of autumn as their climate tends to remain static all year round.

■ Home-made chutney is a deliciously simple way to make the most of the last of summer's tomatoes and apples.

■ The use of the world "fall" rather than autumn is often considered an Americanism. However, fall was actually one of the terms commonly used in Britain for the season between summer and winter until the end of the 17th century, with the French word *autumne* only entering the English language in the 18th century.

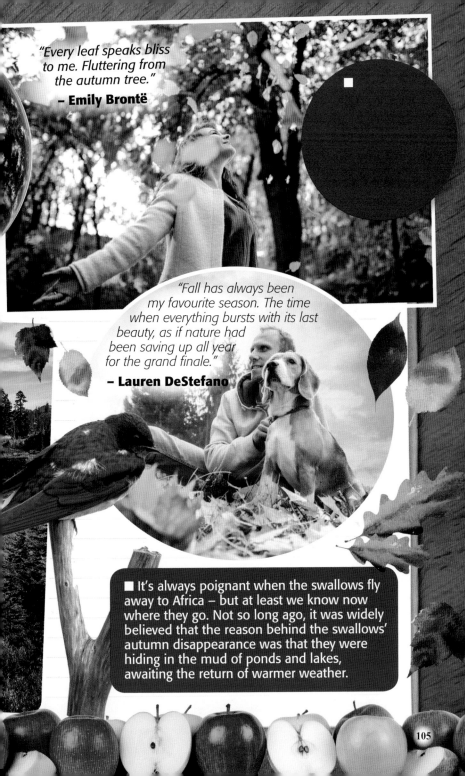

"Every leaf speaks bliss to me. Fluttering from the autumn tree."
– **Emily Brontë**

"Fall has always been my favourite season. The time when everything bursts with its last beauty, as if nature had been saving up all year for the grand finale."
– **Lauren DeStefano**

■ It's always poignant when the swallows fly away to Africa – but at least we know now where they go. Not so long ago, it was widely believed that the reason behind the swallows' autumn disappearance was that they were hiding in the mud of ponds and lakes, awaiting the return of warmer weather.

105

# *Stooks*

WE were probably not more than just two or three,
But the fates mapped the future for Molly and me.
We were taken along to the cornfields each day,
Where our mothers bound sheaves while they watched us at play.

We'd be running and shouting and scaring the rooks
As our fathers were busily building the stooks,
Which, to me, are a symbol of magical days
When we had our first taste of the countryside ways.

In our first years at school we were eager to learn,
But at evenings and weekends were glad to return
To the stooks in the field where we felt really free,
And we played hide and seek until called in for tea.

Then when puberty beckoned, the friendship there'd been
Took another direction – you know what I mean.
On our way home from school we sat down by a stook
And I scrawled *I love you* in her exercise book.

When our schooling was over we worked on the land,
Though we met when we could and we'd stroll hand in hand.
People commented that we were never apart,
But the fact was that Molly had stolen my heart.

We have seen many changes as years have rolled on;
The new tractors have come and the horses have gone
And some strange, modern trends that we couldn't foresee:
There are bales in the fields where the stooks used to be.

As our grandchildren play on a bale in the field.
There's a sense of nostalgia that can't be concealed.
We can watch from our seat in the old inglenook,
But a bale can't compete with the old-fashioned stook.

*– Dennis W. Turner.*

# The House

WHEN evening shadows lengthen, creep,
Across the shuttered little room,
And moonbeams work their faerie skill
On coloured threads to light the gloom,
When night birds break the silent peace
That still enfolds this old, old house,
I lie and listen to the sound
Of little things. I hear a mouse,
I hear the rustle of an owl
Upon her nightly enterprise,
Rain that taps the window-panes,
Wind that fills the room with sighs.
A whispering haunts the quiet house,
Of elms that murmur through the hours,
And each with calming influence
My sense of solitude empowers.
I float with dreams above the clouds,
A sleep which day shall scarcely rouse,
Till morning breaks along the hills
And fills the heart of this old house.

**– *Dawn Lawrence.***

# *Between Time*

THE calendar says autumn and the leaves begin to show
Shades of gold and red in a vivid glorious glow.
The clock tells us it's evening, we give a sigh, begin
To say, checking our watches, "The nights are drawing in!"
And yet, the fragrant roses still perfume the air,
Butterflies still flit and swoop, bees still hover there,
As if the world is pausing, as if time's breath is deep,
And nature is not ready to think of rest and sleep.
It knows and nurtures seasons, it is ready and serene,
But still bestows the beauty of a gentle time between.

*– Deborah Mercer.*

# In The 1930s' Ironmonger's

**A SMELL** assailed my nose today and instantly rolled years away,
Transporting me way back with ease to early childhood memories.
My flight through time came to a stop inside the ironmonger's shop.
I found again a wealth of things from which this little story springs:
The tinkling bell above the door; the well-worn, splintered, boarded floor,
And lots of mousetraps in a bin; the pungent reek of paraffin;
Buckets and enamel bowls; fireside tongs for lifting coals.
Black-lead for the cast-iron hobs; locks and keys and big brass knobs;
Heavy cast-iron cooking pots, flat irons, frying-pans and lots
Of flypapers with sticky glue; Cardinal-Red and Reckitt's Blue;
Tallow candles; garden twine; brushes, paint and turpentine;
The smell of camphor balls for moths pervading towels and kitchen cloths;
Balls of string and lengths of rope; coal-tar and carbolic soap;
The vapours mingling on the air – a unique blend beyond compare.
Tin baths hanging on the walls; dolly-tubs and whitening balls;
Pastry-cutters, rolling pins, baking trays and biscuit tins;
Clothes pegs, washing lines and props; scrubbing brushes, brooms and mops.
Lots of things in rolled-down sacks; nuts and bolts and nails and tacks;
Firewood bundles, neatly stacked; soapflakes – loose or ready packed;
Odours from the soap and sticks all adding to the heady mix.
It was a strange phenomenon and in an instant all was gone.
So be prepared, for none can tell what follows from a simple smell!

*– Dennis W. Turner*

IRONMONGER JD Smith

# Relaxation After Yoga

"**IMAGINE** you are lying
On a sunny tropic beach.
The waves are lapping gently,
The cool shade's within reach."

The voice invites us softly
To drift on fancy's wing,
To mountains, rivers, gardens;
To hear the sweet birds sing.

To ride upon a moonbeam;
To doze beside a fire:
To relax from all the pressures
That trap us in life's mire.

But without the word "imagine",
It doesn't work at all.
I'm lying on the floorboards
Of a draughty village hall!

*– Elizabeth Horrocks.*

# A Day For Ourselves

**H**OW happy can everyone be if we say,
"Let's keep a day for a pottering day"?
A day to do anything, just as we please,
If we want to do nothing, we can be at ease.

How relaxed we feel if we're not chasing time,
To read a good book, when to rest is sublime;
To listen to music, to garden or sew,
Not governed by mealtimes, to go with the flow.

To watch a nice film or to go for a walk,
Take time over coffee, share thoughts and just talk.
To clear out a cupboard, to polish the car,
To sit watching birds feed, content where we are.

A phone call that's promised, a crossword, a nap.
A day when you're able to fill up a gap,
Something you have chosen and so longed to do –
Today is the day, it belongs to just you!

So once in a while have a pottering day,
When work is ignored and routine's pushed away,
Make one day for you, you can share if you must,
Whatever you do, be laid back, don't get fussed.

Then, during the week with the work you must do,
There's always this day you can look forward to,
And when it gets nearer, what pleasure you'll find
In doing whatever is there in your mind.

*– Chrissy Greenslade.*

# Tappity, Tap, Tap

I'VE taken up a hobby;
It comes as a surprise.
When I announce it to my friends
I see it in their eyes!

But I've been to buy my tap shoes –
I'm tapping across the floor!
Things are going swimmingly
As we practise steps once more.

I think I've got the hang of it,
Until the music starts
And then I tie my legs in knots.
Bang! It all falls apart!

The class is sympathetic,
The teacher is so kind,
But my feet are doing what they want
And I'm a tap behind!

Still I'm happy on the back row;
They can't hear me sigh and grunt.
Oh, no! They've all turned round and now
I am at the front!

I guess I'll never be a twinkletoes,
Yet what I have is grit.
This tapper's not for turning
And I will master it!

*– Marian Cleworth.*

# The Colours Of Autumn

**A** **COUPLE** of years ago I holidayed in New England in the autumn. I first went there over 20 years ago, but that was in the summer and I'd always wanted to go back to see the vibrant autumn colours. I wasn't disappointed.

One of the best photographs I took was of a flaming red and orange tree at a viewing point in the White Mountains of New Hampshire with the hills beyond glowing gold into the hazy distance.

People who travel to New England in the "fall" are known as leaf peepers. Of course, they're drawn by the clapboard houses and the coastline, too, but principally it's the colours of the leaves that attracts them.

Isn't it strange how the end of summer, and death and decay, can produce so much beauty? I love the smell of autumn in this country – wet earth and rotting leaves. Everything is closing down for the long bleak stretch of winter, yet it does so with such vibrancy.

It made me think of how we can be something beautiful for God even in the lean and dark times. In fact, these are the very times when we learn what faith really is.

I've recently been reading about the apostle Paul's great vision in his second letter to the Corinthians. He writes about being called up to paradise and hearing and seeing things he could not speak of. Yet something continued to get him down: "A thorn in the flesh, a messenger of Satan to torment me."

He asked God to take it away but God's answer was: "My grace is sufficient for you, for my power is made perfect in weakness."

People often said of Paul: "Who is he? He's got no presence."

And that was the point. Paul didn't want people to think he was magnificent. He wanted them to see the power of God in him, that despite his shortcomings and weaknesses God chose to use him for the growth of the kingdom.

He didn't have an easy time. Again he tells the Corinthians about his sufferings – imprisoned, flogged, stoned, shipwrecked, hungry, thirsty, cold, naked. And yet through it all he has been a witness to the faithfulness of God. Those vibrant ▶

iStock.

*By the Rev. Susan Sarapuk.*

▶ colours of faith have shone through, not because of who he is but because of what God is doing in him.

Do you remember the old days when Hollywood made biblical films from a Christian perspective? In "The Robe", Richard Burton's character is totally bemused that a crippled girl could be content to remain so and find joy in life, and that a little boy to whom he has just given a donkey as a gift could freely give it away to a friend who had more need of it than him.

These people had nothing and yet were happy in their faith, and in the film this has an immense effect on Richard Burton's character.

Modern society does not appreciate weakness and certainly does not celebrate it. Sometimes it seems that those living with disabilities today are sidelined – as if their lives cannot be worth living if they're not fully active. In those circumstances the light and power of God can shine through.

I was watching a programme a while back and it featured a young man who travelled the world talking about his faith. Nothing remarkable about that, except he was born with no arms and legs.

Understandably, as he grew up he became very bitter, knowing that he would never have a normal life. And then Jesus came into his life and he totally transformed it.

He knew then that he was called to be a witness. God has given him this ministry to be an itinerant preacher and God has also blessed him with a wife and family. He is living a vibrant life of faith. What initially had seemed like a decline into decay and the death of hopes and dreams has flared vibrantly into colour.

GOD calls all of us to live vibrant lives of faith in the face of adversity. Often it's those who show faith in the face of extreme events who are the greatest and most effective witnesses. After all, it's easy to talk about faith and how good God is to us when things are going well.

What happens when they're not? Can we still continue to be faithful like Job, who was advised to "Curse God and die", but who instead said that even if God slayed him he would continue to trust? Now that is faith!

"He who began a good work in you will carry it on to completion until the day of Christ Jesus." Philippians 1:6 is one of my favourite verses, because it tells me that life is lived in partnership with God and He's going to make sure I get through.

If I'm struggling I just call out to be helped as Peter did when he began to sink into the waves whilst walking towards Jesus, like the father of the possessed boy who cried out: "I believe, help my unbelief!"

It cannot be summer for ever – no life is lived like that. So when we feel ourselves slipping through autumn towards a period of winter, let's try to make it as spectacular as the colours of a New England fall by continuing to be witnesses to the constancy and love of God. ∎

# A Country Calendar For *Autumn*

"Beautiful things never last. Not roses nor snow . . . And not fireworks, either."
– **Jennifer Donnelly.**

The last Sunday in October marks the end of British Summer Time, when the clocks go back an hour, returning us to Greenwich Mean Time. This first happened in 1916 and proved much more difficult than it is today, as many clock hands only moved in a clockwise direction so going back an hour actually involved moving the clock forward 11 hours.

■ *Hallowe'en can be traced back to the pagan festival of Samhain, which marked the end of summer and the start of winter.*

■ *All over the world, millions of men now grow moustaches in November for Movember, a campaign to highlight and improve men's health.*

■ The fireworks that light up the sky on November 5 were invented in China thousands of years ago – and nine out of ten of all fireworks still come from China.

"Delicious autumn! My very soul is wedded to it, and if I were a bird I would fly about the earth seeking the successive autumns."

**– George Eliot.**

■ *Parkin is one of the treats traditionally associated with Guy Fawkes Night. The recipe for this dark and sticky cake includes treacle, golden syrup, oats and spices – and it's delicious!*

# The River Otter

**H**AVE you ever seen me along the riverside?
It isn't easy to locate those places where I hide.
The den I make is called a holt, but since I am so shy,
There's just a silver bubble trail to show where I've passed by.

But watch: a nose could well appear, then two bright shining eyes,
And a brown face full of whiskers from the water might arise.
I swim as smoothly as an eel; I somersault with ease;
I twist and turn and roll about whichever way I please.

I'll tumble like an acrobat, clap hands with furry paws,
And do all kinds of clever tricks that everyone adores.
I hope you'll catch a glimpse of me – you'll find me a delight.
One day, if you are lucky, you never know, you just might!

*– Dawn Lawrence.*

# Autumn Playtime

**B**ROWN leaves in the ditches, orange on the grass,
Yellow, red are drifting, confetti as we pass.
Golden leaves so crispy, carpeting the wood,
Laughing, trying to catch them, triumphant where we stood.

Crunchy, crispy boot sounds, breathing crisp, cold air,
Gasping at the artistry of colour everywhere.
Autumn! Slanting sunshine dancing through the trees,
Oh, what special memories of childhood days are these!

Laughing as we tossed them, hiding behind trees;
Playtime in the forest, squirrels climb and swing with ease,
Seeking fairy toadstools, tracking hidden deer,
Filled with such excitement at this special time of year.

Remembering the springtime, and summer picnics, too,
Loving forest ponies and hides where we could view
The magic of the forest, today and years ago,
As children wishing next time that we'd play in the snow!

*– Chrissy Greenslade.*

# Bonfire

**T**HE smell of any wood fire smoke,
Or sight of any bonfire blaze
Is always certain to evoke
Old memories of autumn days
When Dad prepared, with rolled-up sleeves,
To tidy up the garden mess.
He raked up heaps of twigs and leaves
And piled them up in readiness.

I watched as Dad prepared a space
Beneath the tangled pile of wood,
And then put kindling in place;
I saw it all from where I stood.
At last the vital moment came
For Dad to get the fire alight.
One match, one strike, one magic flame
And soon the fire was at its height.

Dad added litter carefully,
And flames gave way to drifting smoke.
My eyes were sore; I couldn't see
And I was sure that I would choke.
An orange glow, wood smouldering,
A gusting breeze, a sudden roar;
A snapping, popping, crackling
And sparks and flames began to soar.

And then, when next I saw the scene,
The massive heap had burned away,
And where that raging fire had been
Were smoking ashes, white and grey.
I still recall the smoke-filled air
That swirled, and rose into the skies;
The smoke-filled clothes, the smoke-filled hair
And – most of all – the smoke-filled eyes!

**– Dennis W. Turner.**

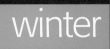

# A Winter's Morning

**O**NE of winter's great delights
Is waking to a world that's white.
Sounds are muffled, views are changed,
And once familiar sights seem strange.
Light reflected off the snow
Creates a truly magical glow,
And there's an other-worldly feel
As nothing now appears quite real.
I think perhaps those sparkles must
Be thanks to a dose of fairy dust,
And marvel at Mother Nature's way
Of granting new wonders every day.

*– Flo Jones.*

# The Tree

FOR well over a hundred years
This tree has been around,
From the day it pushed a brave new shoot
Up through the cold spring ground.

The footpath passing near its roots
Was worn by different shoes;
The tree has heard of wars and deaths
And births and family news.

It's seen the fashions come and go
And change throughout each year;
It's seen the farmland shrinking
And the village creeping near.

It's been the local meeting place,
It's heard of hopes and fears,
And will hold its secrets silently
For another hundred years.

*– Eliza Barret.*

# Perchance To Dream

**W**HEN night-time falls and bedtime calls
I make my way upstairs,
I snuggle deep and wait for sleep
To drive away all cares.
For dreams can shape a sweet escape
To some new place perchance,
Where roses twine and all's set fine
For magic and romance.
But, oh, instead, when I'm in bed
The only dreams I see
Are those of chores, like mopping floors,
Or peeling spuds for tea!
It's so unfair, I quite despair
Of nights of soft guitars,
Still, I'll not mope – I live in hope,
One night I will see stars!

– *Maggie Ingall.*

# Bird's-eye View

O**H**, dear, what a dither, they fly here and thither –
The birds have discovered the suet.
Now they are enlightened and no longer frightened,
At great speed they're all getting through it!

My sparrows are late – I've a family of eight –
Now robin has joined the affray.
He's desperately trying – flaps wings like he's flying –
To hang on, then returns to his tray.

Now down swoop the starlings, for sure not my darlings:
They're quarrelsome and so full of greed,
But robin is singing, he knows food I'm bringing
For his tray as it's his special seed.

Pigeons fully aware that some goodies are there
Are watching and soon will be diving,
But I chase them away from the little birds' tray;
They've eaten and I know they are thriving.

Blackbirds are now pairing, blue tits are sharing,
The feasting we find fascinating,
As our coffee we drink, we know we're on the brink
Of new families we are awaiting.

Then, oh, what a flurry of birds in a hurry
To feed nestlings who are cheeping and tweeting.
I'm so glad to say that I've helped them today,
As birdwatching for me takes some beating.

*– Chrissy Greenslade.*

139

# The Rug Makers

**C**ARPETS were a rarity in Grandma's living-room;
Just brightly coloured, pegged rag rugs and brown linoleum.
Grandma made the rugs herself on a wooden pegging frame
With cogs to turn the canvas and keep all the rows the same.
No visitors at Grandma's were allowed to slack or shirk –
She'd hand out pairs of scissors and old cloth coats and skirts.
They'd cut them into narrow strips, three inches wide – no more.
And then again to little bits, hands blistered, red and sore.
It was never very tidy whenever visitors called.
There would be piles of woolly pegging bits, all heaped against the wall.

There were no bouncy castles then, or fancy trampolines –
Just lovely, bouncy pegging bits of reds and blues and greens.
We'd mix them up, pile them up, a multicoloured heap.
We'd jump in them, lie in them, sometimes fall asleep.
The grown-ups would be busy, working at the frame:
Peg a row, turn the cog, peg a row again.
Sometimes they'd be adventurous, start a brand-new trend:
Diamond in the middle, patterns at each end.
If they should take a tea break, we kids would have a go,
Pegging childhood memories into every row.

The rug makers have passed on now and really it's a shame
That none of us know what became of Grandma's pegging frame.

*– Glenice Crossland.*

141

# from the Manse Window

## Time After Time

I WAS ordained in West Kirk Presbyterian Church on Belfast's Shankill Road in the winter month of January 1990. Some years back, to mark 20 years of ordained ministry, my wife and family gave me a most beautiful gift.

It is a Swiss-made, "half-hunter" pocket watch, complete with silver chain. I carry it to church on special occasions in my waistcoat pocket. Now, it's not waterproof, solar-powered or digital. It doesn't record laptimes or give altitude. It has a face and hands, needs to be wound manually and ticks very loudly. I guess it's kind of "old school" but hey, it's got class.

I remember the elderly jeweller and watch repairer who brought it out to show to us. He was a real enthusiast, whose shop with its wood panelling and glass and loudly ticking clocks on most of the walls almost constituted an antique in itself! Tucked away in his cramped, almost Dickensian workshop, hidden behind the shop counter, he used to love opening the back of old watches to study the mechanism with a custom magnifying lens. It seemed to give him great pleasure when

iStock.

everything was well-made and in order, ticking along correctly.

"There's one with a lovely movement," he would murmur with approval. He was one of a dwindling few who was able to follow and appreciate the workings of such things.

For all the information available in the world these days, many struggle to find any order or reason to life. While we can have instant access via the internet to encyclopaedic detail on just about every imaginable subject, life itself can remain an incomprehensible, and often painful, mystery. Vandalism and crime, disaster, illness and tragedy continue daily, all with no apparent purpose. The world appears in frustratingly random chaos, without rhyme nor reason.

But the Maker does give us signposts to help us find our way. We do get slipped some pointers – if we're willing to see them. We might consider some amazing mechanisms in nature, like the solar system, photosynthesis, the tides or the seasons. Albert Einstein was not a conventionally religious man, yet this widely acknowledged genius expressed humble ▶

*By the Rev. Andrew Watson.*

▶ wonder at the order he observed in the universe.

And what about the complexities of the human body – the respiratory system, the circulation, the immune or nervous systems? Sometimes it's only when we need a trip to the doctor or the hospital that we appreciate how wonderfully made we are.

Then again, sometimes we experience amazing "coincidental" circumstances which seem like an answer to the prayer we perhaps hadn't even got around to making yet. Such occasions make us feel that maybe there is somebody up there who does actually see and care.

Oh, and then there's that inner sense (admittedly stronger some days than others) when we are trusting, following and trying to obey Christ – that there is a plan. Some kind of big picture. A comforting assurance that the One Who Knows and understands and actually runs the mechanisms of the universe knows what He's doing and more, has a part for us to play.

Of course there's always Jesus – wise, kind, gentle, awe-inspiring, daunting yet captivating – I could go on. His unique combination of moral perfection and deep compassion; his motives so pure; his love so undeserved. Grace, they call it in the bible.

Surely the bible itself is another clearly ordered message, pointing us to the source from whom all life has come and to whom we will all one day return. Psalm 19 celebrates both the daily natural sunlight and the Commandments God has given for our moral and spiritual enlightenment. These rules and guidelines give light and order for individuals, families and communities!

In fact the bible contains 66 separate written works, written over a thousand years by a range of authors, fiercely preserved with impeccable accuracy, having one unifying theme and one central character, Jesus Christ, Son of God.

Engraved on the back of my presentation watch is a bible reference – Ephesians 2 v10. After spelling out how Christians have been rescued to enjoy new life by God's grace through trusting in Jesus, the Apostle Paul emphasises that it's really the Lord's doing, not ours.

"For we are God's workmanship, created in Christ Jesus to do good works which God prepared in advance for us to do."

I suppose that could sound a bit mysterious, or even intimidating. Many feel underqualified to serve Christ and are hesitant to step forward in case he asks us to do something outside our comfort zone.

But in actual fact it is much more reassuring! We could never correctly please him, much less evangelise the world or build his church in our own limited strength. We need his spirit to fill and empower us, his wisdom to guide our words and actions. Above all, we need his generous love motivating our hearts with his concern, prompting us to treat others as we ourselves would like to be treated.

While at times we may feel very much like a work in progress, we are,

nevertheless, God's workmanship. He has recreated us in the likeness of his son and is at work in us still to fulfil his good purposes.

This is not to be understood as something exceptional or out of the ordinary. It's just what the Maker intends for now. It's just how things are meant to be when they're ticking along correctly.

Just like this beautiful timepiece. ■

# A Country Calendar For *Winter*

■ The Chinese Plum is one of the few flowers that blossoms in winter. Mainly grown in Asia, this delicate flower is considered a symbol of good luck, prosperity and longevity.

■ Christmas cake as we know it is actually a combination of two festive delicacies: plum pottage, a porridge-type dish traditionally eaten on Christmas Eve in mediaeval days, and its 16th-century replacement, which swapped oatmeal for butter, flour, eggs and dried fruit. This rich cake became today's Christmas cake after innovative cooks added spices to the mixture, then covered the finished cake in marzipan and, later, icing.

■ Squirrels don't hibernate in winter. They simply refuse to leave the comfort of their cosy nests, tucking into the nuts they stored away in autumn, only venturing into the snow if supplies run low.

■ On average, a snowflake falls to the ground at a speed of three miles per hour.

■ On Christmas Eve, it's been calculated that Santa Claus visits 5,556 homes per second as he delivers gifts to the world's 1.6 billion children. That's a lot of chimneys to climb down! And even more mince-pies to eat!

# *Sharing*

**I** **LOVE** to sit in the sunshine; I like to walk in the rain.
It's great to be out on a windy day and be blown back home again.
I like a slice of buttered toast; I love a piece of cake,
And it's grand to be in the kitchen when bread is in to bake.

If we can be the sunshine when others walk in rain;
If we can be the welcome home when friends are feeling pain;
If we can share life's pleasures with folk who find things tough –
It may be a small, small thing to do, but it just might be enough.

***– Norman Lindsey.***

# Anniversary Waltz

THEY'D said they'd spend it quietly:
"Just a night in, you and me."
Their gifts were simple. "There's no sense
In going to too much expense!"
They'd both agreed on that, and yet,
She gave a soft sigh of regret
As the evening hours slipped by –
And yes, he heard, and he knew why!
He took out that CD he'd found
After he had looked around
In shops, on websites, hours, days long
Until, at last, he'd traced "their song".
It never reached the hit parade,
Even back then was rarely played,
But something in them seemed to chime
With its lilting 3/4 time,
With its gentle harmony.
He asked her, "Care to dance with me?"
And then, as if by magic, they
Were dancing all the years away.

– *Deborah Mercer.*

# *An Empty Page*

**A**N empty page is always looked upon by someone who's been bitten,
As a fascinating story that is waiting to be written.
They can see the stark, white blankness and the longer their gaze lingers
There's more wild imagination and more twitching of the fingers.

It's a scene of crime where criminals can carry out their missions;
It's a trysting place where timid lovers lose their inhibitions;
It's a courtroom where the barrister is cleverly defending;
It's the setting for a sorry tale that needs a happy ending.

It's a cyberspace where sci-fi tales defy imagination,
Or a thousand other stories of the author's own creation.
Then the characters are conjured up to populate the stage
That was once a plain and innocent and simple empty page.

*– Dennis W. Turner.*

# Memories Galore

**W**HERE do you keep your mementoes,
Old keepsakes and prized souvenirs?
So often they're found all around us,
Just waiting to take us back years.

Are photographs kept in an album,
Or proudly displayed on the wall?
Perhaps there's a song or a perfume
That prompts you to fondly recall.

And maybe you kept old recordings:
You sit and watch past times unfold
Of families or special occasions –
Memories more precious than gold.

Did you keep books from your childhood?
Do you happen upon them and read?
Transport yourself back to your young days –
Sweet echoes of peace guaranteed.

Perhaps there's an item of jewellery;
A gift to you from someone dear.
Do you wear it or look at it often
To keep distant memories near?

Such comforting little reminders!
So many to treasure and store.
We cherish those times of reflection
When keepsakes bring memories galore.

*– Emma Canning.*

# *Fibber!*

THE camera doesn't lie –
That's what we're always told.
But if that's really true,
Then why do I look old?
The person in this pic
Looks elderly and grey,
It doesn't show the Me
That hasn't gone away.
The Me who lives inside,
Who may have passed eighteen,
But who still loves her life,
Who's positive and keen.
There's still new folk to meet,
New places to explore,
So much to do and see –
This world could never bore!
So though, in terms of years,
I might look overdone,
The camera does tell lies –
I've really just begun!

*– Maggie Ingall.*

# Kindness, Love And Hope

**W**E all have worries in our lives
And problems great and small,
And as we journey on our way
We stumble and we fall.
But now and then we're lifted up
By just a kindly word,
And sometimes smiles will touch the heart
And once more hope is stirred.

We all have sadness in our lives
And times of doubt and fears,
But love is there to guard and guide
And wipe away the tears.
When you find kindness, love and hope
Don't let them slip away,
These precious gifts will make you strong
So cherish them each day.

**– Iris Hesselden.**

# Mother

**W**HAT is a mother when you're very small?
A sweet-scented cushion, a protective stone wall;
A skirt to cling on to and hide from the world;
A bosom to sleep on, a kiss and a curl;
A frown that can shame you when you're in disgrace;
A sparkle to bring back the smile to your face;
A teller of stories, a nurse and a clown;
Arms to uplift you, when you are down;
A goddess, an angel, the best mum of all –
That is a mother when you're very small.

What is a mother when you're in your teens?
A horror who patches your new kneeless jeans,
Who thinks that by midnight you should be in bed;
Who knows what you're thinking, sees inside your head;
Invades your room at least once a day,
Moves things, irons things, throws things away.
Thinks all your friends are wild or uncouth;
Compares today with the days of her youth;
Nags and embarrasses without any cause;
Even blames you for her own menopause.

What is a mother when you're growing old?
A friend and a mentor more precious than gold;
A woman with wisdom she's gained through the years,
Who's learned to survive all the trouble and tears;
Who knits endless woollies to keep us all warm,
And when there's a crisis is gentle and calm.
Someone to watch over, care for each day;
The first one we think of, each time we pray;
What is a mother when we have to part?
A sweet, loving memory, deep in our heart.

– *Glenice Crossland.*

# A Light Shining Through

"THE dark night wakes, the glory breaks, and Christmas comes once more."

These words form the closing lines of a rarely sung verse of one of our most well-loved carols, "O Little Town of Bethlehem". And for me – even so many years on from childhood – they continue to stir the imagination and send a delicious shiver of anticipation down my spine.

My early experience of the "dark night" attaches itself to clear memories of the seemingly endless dark hours of early Christmas morning. My younger sister and I – both of us wide awake after midnight communion and now sleepless from excitement – waited impatiently for the time when our parents had said we could open our stockings. Had Father Christmas come? Of course he had! The long wait was at last over, and Christmas had "come once more".

Yet the words of the hymn have a much wider and more contemporary application. They remind us that in a pain-torn, war-weary world the eternal message of Christmas continues to shine as a beacon of hope. Even in

our day when the rampant spread of secularism and consumerism often seems to be unstoppable, many people – to their surprise, perhaps – still find themselves touched and moved by the events surrounding the stable in Bethlehem.

The dark night referred to in the carol was not a new thing – it had been a very long night indeed. Some five or six centuries before the birth of Christ, the Old Testament author of the book of Isaiah wrote: "The people who walked in darkness have seen a great light; those who lived in a land of deep darkness – on them the light has shined . . . For a child has been born to us, a son given to us . . ." (Isaiah 9:2, 6-7).

I'm sure it won't be just the singers amongst us who hear Isaiah's words set to Handel's evocative music in his oratorio "Messiah". Handel structured his work to show that this prophecy pointed clearly to the birth of Jesus, but the original writer would have known nothing of that event in the distant future.

Isaiah's words originally emerged from a time of loss

*iStock.*

By the Rev. Barbara Mosse.

▶ and despair for the Israelite people. Driven out of their homeland by their enemies, they had been condemned to many generations of foreign exile, yet the beacon of hope for their eventual return was never fully extinguished.

In Handel's music the first phrase, usually sung by a rich bass voice, winds sinuously around the singer's lower register, graphically depicting a people stumbling around, lost in the darkness. Then the music rises and blossoms out as the light dawns with the promise of restoration.

The words of the ecstatic, joy-filled chorus "For unto us a child is born" are thought to have originally been written to celebrate the birth of a new king, holding out further promise and hope for the future. But as the centuries continued to pass, church tradition came to see this prophecy as achieving its deepest and most richly textured meaning in the ultimate royal birth, that of the Christ-child in Bethlehem.

So far, we've travelled a long way backwards in time, and we've moved about quite a bit. From two excited children waiting impatiently for the dawn of Christmas morning we moved forward to the present, and glimpsed the seeds of hope and longing amidst the consumerism and secularism of our present world. Then we plunged back into history, to the words of Isaiah and the suffering and hope of the Israelite people in exile.

And now the Gospel of John takes us further back still, into the mysterious workings of God in the dizzying, unimaginable mists that precede the dawn of history:

"In the beginning was the Word, and the Word was with God, and the Word was God . . . All things came into being through him . . . What has come into being through him was life, and the life was the life of all people. The light shines in the darkness, and the darkness did not overcome it" (John 1:1, 3-5).

Here, in the time before time, we are in a place of mystery, poetry and John's divinely inspired spiritual imagination. You won't find any description of the Bethlehem stable in John; after this wonderful opening to his gospel he moves directly to the meeting between the adult Jesus and his cousin John the Baptist, and the start of Jesus's public ministry.

But for the gospel-writer, the Word, whom we meet first as the baby of Bethlehem, is none other than the Christ, the Word and Wisdom of God from all eternity, and the divine channel through whom all creation comes into being. It is mind-stretching; breathtaking. And just when our minds are threatening to collapse under the enormity of it all, John tells us that "the Word became flesh and lived among us, and we have seen his glory . . . as of a father's only son, full of grace and truth" (John 1:14). The cosmic and unimaginable becomes homely and familiar; he lives amongst humans and reaches out in love, healing and forgiveness to all those who for centuries had longed to welcome him.

And what about us, today? How do we recognise, and respond to, our own inner longing and yearning? It is wonderful to be able to worship Jesus, the

baby in the manger, at Christmastime. But do we also expect to meet him on every other day of the year, in the tapestry of joy and sorrow, pain and delight that makes up every human life? Just as our faith encourages us to recognise the presence of the risen Christ in our lives each day, so, too, it challenges us to invite the infant Christ to take up permanent residence in our hearts. We have come full circle, to the final verse of the beautiful carol where we began our journey:

"O Holy Child of Bethlehem, descend to us, we pray;
Cast out our sin and enter in, be born in us today." ∎

# A Country Calendar For *Winter*

■ To help ensure your Christmas poinsettia lasts, place the plant in daylight but out of the reach of direct sunlight and keep it clear of draughts. It's important not to overwater poinsettias, so only water when the surface of the soil has dried out – and place the pot on a tray of gravel or pebbles to encourage good drainage.

■ Looking through a microscope, no two snowflakes are the same, but they all have one thing in common: six sides.

"Winter is the time for comfort, for good food and warmth, for the touch of a friendly hand and for a talk beside the fire: it is the time for home."

**– Edith Sitwell**

■ According to folklore, if a girl sees a sparrow on Valentine's Day, she'll marry a poor man – but if she spots a goldfinch, she'll marry a millionaire!

■ In Madrid, Spain, New Year revellers celebrate the start of the New Year by eating 12 grapes as the church bells strike midnight on December 31, with each grape promising good luck in a different month of the year.

■ Turquoise is the birthstone for December, garnet (which comes in black and green as well as red) is the birthstone for January, while February's birthstone is the purple or violet amethyst.

"For last year's words belong to last year's language And next year's words await another voice. And to make an end is to make a beginning."

**– T.S. Eliot**

168

# Memory Benches

**I**N certain beauty spots round here
Are benches with a small brass plate,
All welcome as a place to rest,
Each one there to commemorate
And keep alive the memory
Of loved ones now no longer here,
But whose bright spirits still live on
In places that they once held dear.

I often breathe a silent thanks
For those whose lives have gone before,
For each carved name, familiar now,
Is like a friend I see no more.

*– Eileen Hay.*

# *Life Journey*

**W**<sup>E</sup> gather round the manger with Mary, shepherds, kings,
For we have heard the message, the breath of angels' wings.
Our hearts rejoice with Mary, our spirits soar above,
For in her tiny baby dwells God's perfect gift of love.

And now the scene is changing, and a cross is lifted high,
While Mary stands beside her son the scoffers pass on by.
Will we still stay with Mary? Will we now share her pain?
Will we hold fast beside the cross till Easter comes again?

The miracle has happened, and Jesus lives once more!
And Mary dwells amongst his friends, her Saviour to adore.
Do we still stand with Mary? Can we embrace all things
God gifts to us: our lives, our hope, the joy in all he brings?

**– Barbara Mosse.**

## *January Sales*

CHRISTMAS now has been and gone
And all that it entails,
And so the next event in store
Is the January sales.
There will be so many bargains
Designed to melt the heart,
So I'm really looking forward to
The day that they all start.

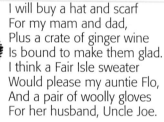

I will buy a hat and scarf
For my mam and dad,
Plus a crate of ginger wine
Is bound to make them glad.
I think a Fair Isle sweater
Would please my auntie Flo,
And a pair of woolly gloves
For her husband, Uncle Joe.

I'll buy myself a toaster
And a heater (fan),
And a brand-new walking stick
For my dear old gran.
For, on consideration and when
All's been done and said,
When Christmas comes around again,
I'll be a year ahead!

*– Brian H. Gent.*

"The only way to have a
friend is to be one."
– *Ralph Waldo Emerson.*